DISCOVER DOGS WITH THE AMERICAN CANINE ASSOCIATION

I LIKE AUSTRALIAN SHEPHERDS!

Linda Bozzo

It is the mission of the American Canine Association (ACA) to provide registered dog owners with the educational support needed for raising, training, showing, and breeding the healthiest pets expected by responsible pet owners throughout the world. Through our activities and services, we encourage and support the dog world in order to promote best-known husbandry standards as well as to ensure that the voice and needs of our customers are quickly and properly addressed.

Our continued support, commitment, and direction are guided by our customers, including veterinary, legal, and legislative advisors. ACA aims to provide the most efficient, cooperative, and courteous service to our customers and strives to set the standard for education and problem solving for all who depend on our services.

For more information, please visit www.acacanines.com, email customerservice@acadogs.com, phone 1-800-651-8332, or write to the American Canine Association at PO Box 121107, Clermont, FL 34712.

Published in 2018 by Enslow Publishing, LLC.
101 W. 23rd Street, Suite 240, New York, NY 10011

Library of Congress Cataloging-in-Publication Data

Names: Bozzo, Linda, author.
Title: I like Australian shepherds! / Linda Bozzo.
Description: New York : Enslow Publishing, 2018. | Series: Discover dogs with the American Canine Association | Includes bibliographical references and index. | Audience: Grades K to 3.
Identifiers: LCCN 2017001302| ISBN 9780766086340 (library-bound) | ISBN 9780766088733 (pbk.) | ISBN 9780766088672 (6-pack)
Subjects: LCSH: Australian shepherd dog—Juvenile literature.
Classification: LCC SF429.A79 B69 2017 | DDC 636.737—dc23
LC record available at https://lccn.loc.gov/2017001302

Printed in the United States of America

To Our Readers: We have done our best to make sure all websites in this book were active and appropriate when we went to press. However, the author and the publisher have no control over and assume no liability for the material available on those websites or on any websites they may link to. Any comments or suggestions can be sent by email to customerservice@enslow.com.

Photo Credits: Cover, p. 1 cynoclub/Shutterstock.com; p. 3 (left) Stanislav Duben/Shutterstock.com; p. 3 (right) Mark Herreid/Shutterstock.com; p. 5 Grigorita Ko/Shutterstock.com; p. 6 Juniors Bildarchiv GmbH/Alamy Stock Photo; p. 9 © iStockphoto.com/Treiderbest; p. 10 cynoclub/Thinkstock; pp. 13 (left), 18 © iStockphoto.com/GlobalP; p. 13 (collar) graphicphoto/iStock/Thinkstock, (bed) Luisa Leal Photography/Shutterstock.com, (brush) gvictoria/Shutterstock.com, (food and water bowls) exopixel/Shutterstock.com, (leash, toys) © iStockphoto.com/Liliboas; p. 14 Jennie Book/Shutterstock.com; p. 17 Mark Raycroft/Minden Pictures/Getty Images; p. 19 absolutimages/Shutterstock.com; p. 21 Theresa Martinez.

Enslow Publishing
101 W. 23rd Street
Suite 240
New York, NY 10011
USA
enslow.com

CONTENTS

IS AN AUSTRALIAN SHEPHERD RIGHT FOR YOU? 4

A DOG OR A PUPPY? 7

LOVING YOUR AUSTRALIAN SHEPHERD 8

EXERCISE 11

FEEDING YOUR AUSTRALIAN SHEPHERD 12

GROOMING 15

WHAT YOU SHOULD KNOW 16

A GOOD FRIEND 19

NOTE TO PARENTS 20

WORDS TO KNOW 22

READ ABOUT DOGS 23

INDEX 24

IS AN AUSTRALIAN SHEPHERD RIGHT FOR YOU?

Australian shepherds, also known as **Aussies**, can make great family dogs. But they are not a good choice for first-time dog owners.

Aussies need lots of room to run. If you live in the country, an Aussie might be right for you.

Australian shepherds are actually an American breed.

A DOG OR A PUPPY?

Aussie puppies need slow, firm training. If you do not have time to train a puppy, an older Aussie may be better for your family.

Your Aussie will grow to be medium to large in size.

Aussies need company.

LOVING YOUR AUSTRALIAN SHEPHERD

Love your Aussie by spending lots of time with him. Teach him tricks. Take him to the park where he will have lots of space to run. He likes to learn and keep busy!

EXERCISE

Aussies need lots of playtime and long walks on a **leash**. This dog is always ready to play games, like **fetch**.

Australian shepherds can get bored easily. If left alone too long, your Aussie may bark and get into trouble.

FEEDING YOUR AUSTRALIAN SHEPHERD

Aussies can be fed wet or dry dog food. Ask a **veterinarian (vet)**, a doctor for animals, which food is best for your dog and how much to feed her. Give your Aussie fresh, clean water every day.

Remember to keep your dog's food and water dishes clean. Dirty dishes can make a dog sick.

Do not feed your dog people food. It can make her sick.

Your new dog will need:

a collar with a tag

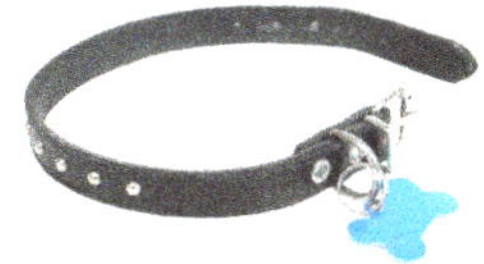

a bed

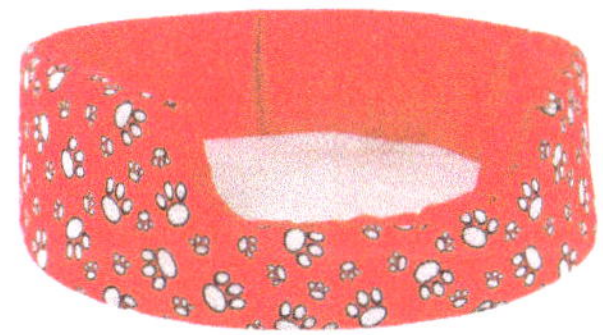

a brush

food and water dishes

a leash

toys

Aussies can have straight or curly coats.

GROOMING

Aussies **shed** all year long. This means their hair falls out all the time. Aussies need to be brushed to keep them clean and looking their best.

Your dog will need a bath every so often. Use a gentle soap made just for dogs. An Aussie's nails need to be clipped. A vet or **groomer** can show you how. Your dog's ears should be cleaned and his teeth should be brushed by an adult.

WHAT YOU SHOULD KNOW

Aussies don't do well with small pets or cats because they might try to **herd** them.

Aussies are not good for busy families because they need to be around people.

Aussies are happiest when they have a job to do.

Aussies were bred to herd livestock.

You will need to take your new dog to the vet for a checkup. He will need shots, called **vaccinations**, and yearly checkups to keep him healthy. If you think your dog may be sick or hurt, call your vet.

A GOOD FRIEND

Like a good friend, your Aussie will want to be by your side. These gentle dogs can live as long as 15 years.

NOTE TO PARENTS

It is important to consider having your dog spayed or neutered when the dog is young. Spaying and neutering are operations that prevent unwanted puppies and can help improve the overall health of your dog.

It is also a good idea to microchip your dog, in case he or she gets lost. A vet will implant a microchip under the skin containing an identification number that can be scanned at a vet's office or animal shelter. The microchip registry is contacted, and the company uses the ID number to look up your information from a database.

Some towns require licenses for dogs, so be sure to check with your town clerk.

For more information, speak with a vet.

There are many dogs, young and old, waiting to be adopted from animal shelters and rescue groups.

Words to Know

Aussie Another name for an Australian shepherd.

fetch To go after a toy and bring it back.

groomer A person who bathes and brushes dogs.

herd To gather and keep in a group.

leash A chain or strap that attaches to a dog's collar.

shed When dog hair falls out so new hair can grow.

vaccinations Shots that dogs need to stay healthy.

veterinarian (vet) A doctor for animals.

Read About Dogs

Books

Brown, Domini. *Australian Shepherds* (Awesome Dogs). Minnetonka, MN: Bellweather Media, Inc., 2017.

Gunderson, Megan. *Australian Shepherds* (Dogs). Minneapolis, MN: Abdo Publishing, 2013.

McKenzie, Precious. *Australian Shepherds* (Dog Applause). Vero Beach, FL: Rourke Pub Group, 2017.

Websites

American Canine Association Inc., Kids Corner

www.acakids.com

Visit the official website of the American Canine Association.

National Geographic Kids, Pet Central

kids.nationalgeographic.com/explore/pet-central/

Learn more about dogs and other pets at the official site of the National Geographic Society for Kids.

INDEX

B
bathing, 15
bed, 13
brush/brushing, 13, 15

D
dishes, 12, 13

F
family, 4, 16
fetch, 11
food, 12, 13

G
groomer, 15

H
herding, 16

L
leash, 11, 13
lifespan, 19

M
microchip, 20

N
nails

O
older dogs, 7

P
playtime, 11
puppies, 7

R
running, 4, 8

S
shedding, 15
size, 7
spaying/neutering, 20
supplies, 13

T
toys, 13
training, 7
tricks, 8

V
vet, 12, 20

W
walks, 11
water, 12, 13